CHRONICLE BOOKS
SAN FRANCISCO

amphibians&reptiles IN 3-D

mark blum

acknowledgments

I am grateful to the following individuals and businesses for their roles in helping to bring this book to completion: Dan Blodget (SubAquatic Camera Repair Company), Walter Broda, Danny Chan (Dances with Snakes), Charles Debono (Mad Jungle Reptiles), Fry Photographics, Gecko Ranch, Mary Henness, Robert Kandell (Shutterbug Shop), Stephen and Dennis Karmann (Rainforest Pet Shop), Matthew Marion, Jose Oseguera and John DiGirolamo (Peninsula Aquatic Habitats), A. A. Pennings, Charles Powell II, Ben and Laura Skeen (Picture Perfect Pets), Sandra Spoden (Frogs-n-Stuff), and Western Zoological Supply. I especially thank Marian, Ryan, and Lauren Blum for providing the love and support that nurtures my photographic passions.

Library of Congress Cataloging-in-Publication Data:
    Blum, Mark.
    Amphibians & reptiles in 3-D / by Mark Blum.
        p. cm.
    Includes index.
    ISBN 0-8118-2509-4
    1. Reptiles. 2. Amphibians. 3. Reptiles—Pictorial works.
4. Amphibians—Pictorial works. 5. Stereoscopic views.   I. Title.
II. Title: Amphibians and reptiles in 3-D.
    QL641.B58   1999
    597.9'022'2—dc21   99-18128
                                        CIP

Printed in Hong Kong.

Designed by Julia Flagg

Distributed in Canada by Raincoast Books
8680 Cambie Street
Vancouver, British Columbia V6P 6M9

10 9 8 7 6 5 4 3 2

Chronicle Books
85 Second Street
San Francisco, California 94105

www.chroniclebooks.com

preface

The first book to be published exclusively on the subject of amphibians and reptiles was a volume produced in 1640 by the Italian naturalist Aldrovanus; a work which was illustrated with woodcut prints. The book you hold in your hands is also unique: the first book with built-in stereoscopic lenses dedicated solely to these extraordinary creatures. You have only to view the 3-D plates in this book first with one eye closed, and then with both eyes open, to appreciate the truer sense of each animal's appearance revealed by the three-dimensional image pair.

Herpetologists have identified roughly 6,500 species of reptiles and amphibians. While this collection of 44 images presents only a small sampling, I have selected animals that give a sense of the astonishing array of species living on earth today.

For the last 300 years, the identification and study of living things has been aided immensely by an orderly system of nomenclature developed by Swedish scientist Carolus Linnaeus. Under this taxonomic system, all living things are classified by a two-part name: the genus, usually a Greek word or derivative, used to describe a group of closely related plants or animals; and the species, normally a Latin derivative, the name given to lifeforms so closely related that they can interbreed. Sometimes the species are further broken down into subspecies, usually based on geographical distribution. These scientific names have been used to precisely identify each animal on the following pages. Common names are also provided, but these are not standardized and a species may have many different common names, or none at all.

When I set out to photograph this work, I knew that it would be different from all my previous books, which were primarily shot on location in the wild. Due to practical constraints, capturing images representative of the great diversity of reptiles and amphibians spread around the globe meant photographing many animals in captivity. I initially approached this task with some trepidation, expecting to find animals callously exported from their native lands, little understood and poorly cared for. Happily, this was not the case. By and large I found knowledgeable retailers, hobbyists, and herptoculturists dedicated to responsible animal husbandry and captive breeding programs. The vast majority of reptiles and amphibians sold in the United States are born in captivity, not exported from their homelands. In fact, the most sought-after species are often hybrids or color morphs that may not even exist in the wild. Regardless of one's opinion about the keeping of animals in captivity, from an ecological perspective it's far better that captive specimens not be taken from their native habitats.

The export of wild animals for sale to the general public is a bad practice for a host of reasons. Wild captured animals are often taken and cared for indiscriminately, resulting in extremely high mortality rates, the imbalancing of native populations, and ultimately the disruption of local ecology. Those animals that actually make it to the retail markets are frequently ridden with parasites—a burden they can easily tolerate in the wild, but which can quickly kill them under the stressful conditions of export and captivity. Professional herptoculturists have methods for purging wild specimens of parasites that are beyond the means of the average retailer or pet owner. For all of these reasons, persons interested in keeping reptiles or amphibians should insist on animals that have been born in captivity.

The question of exporting is not entirely black and white, however. The responsible export of wild reptiles and amphibians for the purpose of captive breeding programs may serve to perpetuate many threatened species. This is especially true in the tropics, where export pressures are particularly intense and native habitats are being disrupted or eliminated at alarming rates. Hopefully, this book will not only entertain, but also inspire readers to a greater understanding and appreciation of reptiles, amphibians, and the environmental conditions crucial to their survival.

(Readers interested in purchasing a hands-free table top viewer for the 3-D books in this series may obtain details by sending a self-addressed stamped envelope to Mark Blum, P. O. Box 3350, Monterey, CA USA 93942-3350).

THE plates

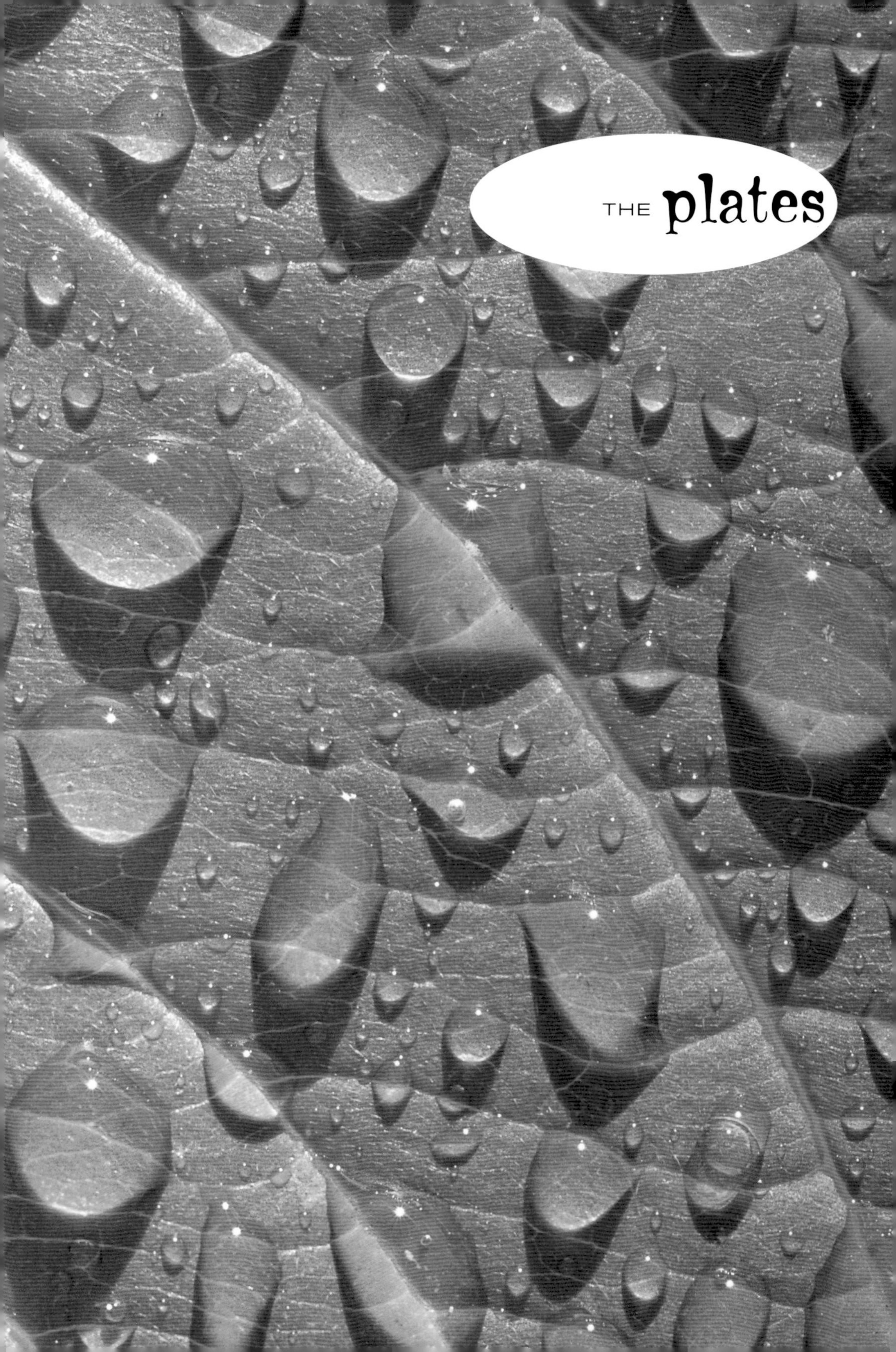

plate 1

chacoan monkey frog

PHYLLOMEDUSA SAUVAGII

SOUTH AMERICAN GRAN CHACO

This unusual frog is highly adapted for life in the hot, arid climate of the Gran Chaco area of South America. Possessed of opposable first fingers and toes for grasping, the Chacoan monkey frog is an excellent climber. It conserves water loss by several unique methods, including secreting a waxy substance that covers the skin. If ambient temperatures exceed 104 degrees Fahrenheit, the Chacoan monkey frog can cool down by letting water droplets form on its skin. It also excretes uric acid in semisolid form and reabsorbs water through its bladder. This exceptional combination of adaptive features reduces water loss to a level found in many desert lizards, just 10 percent of that in most other frogs. The Chacoan monkey frog's distribution includes southeast Bolivia, northwest Argentina, and much of Paraguay.

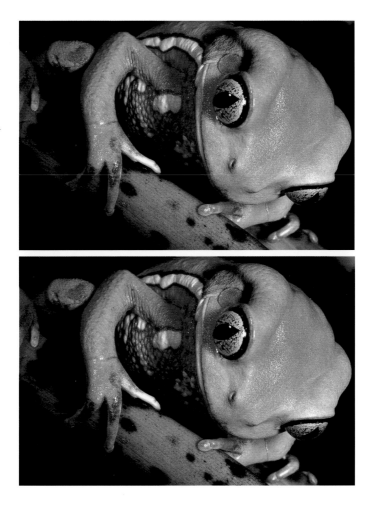

plate 2

california (lavender) king snake

LAMPROPELTIS GETULAE CALIFORNIAE

CALIFORNIA

Like the king cobra, the king snake's common name derives from its practice of eating other snakes, including venomous species. Incredibly, consuming the deadly snake toxins does not harm the king snake. King snakes display enormous variation in coloration and patterning. Even among the same species, there are many different phases. The snake in this picture is not a naturally occurring phase, but a hybrid developed by snake breeders, known as the lavender king snake.

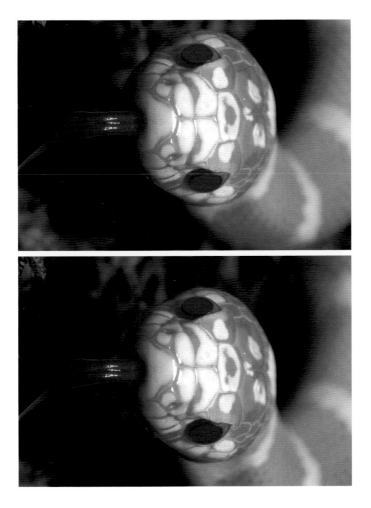

plate 3

montane horned lizard

ACANTHOSAURA ARMATA

SOUTHEAST ASIA

These Old World lizards are members of the family Agamidae. Agamids are generally robust with a large head and a long tail that cannot be discarded. They are heavily scaled and sometimes have spines, as does this specimen. Agamids rely more on their excellent vision than on their sense of smell. They mainly feed on arthropods. The montane horned lizard and other members of the genus *Acanthosaura* occupy mountain forests from southern China to Sumatra. Like the chameleons, they have the remarkable ability to change their coloration in response to behavioral stimuli.

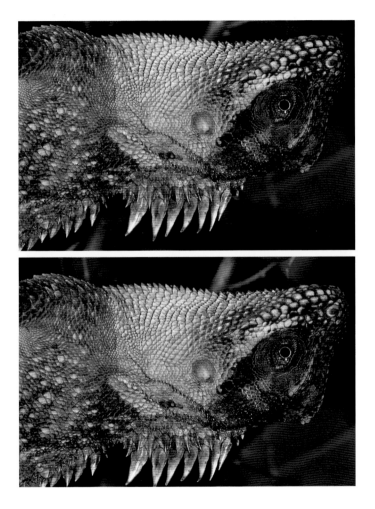

plate 4

blue poison-dart frog

DENDROBATES AZURES

REPUBLIC OF SURINAME

The brilliant blue coloration displayed by this striking blue poison-dart frog is rare in nature. This creature is one of about 135 species forming a group of small, brightly colored frogs from Central and South America. Known as Dendrobatid frogs, they are often referred to as "jewels of the rain-forest." Four genera of Dendrobatid frogs are poisonous in varying degrees, including this genus, *Dendrobates*. For untold centuries, the native hunters of Central and South America have applied the lethal secretions from several of the most poisonous of these frogs to their blowgun darts, engendering the common name. The blue poison-dart frog is endemic to the Republic of Suriname on the northeast coast of South America.

plate 5

emperor newt

TYLOTOTRITON VERRUCOSUS

WESTERN AND CENTRAL ASIA

This newt is named "emperor" for the crownlike appearance of its heavily armored skull. It is also known as the Mandarin salamander or crocodile newt, and is native to the mountains of western China, Nepal, Burma, Thailand, and northern India. The thick bones of the crown and the orange bumps along the ribs discourage predators, as do chemical repellents in the skin. Even so, the newt is eaten by water snakes and birds of prey, and is nocturnally active to reduce the risk of predation. Fertilization takes place externally. After a one- to three-week development period, females deposit their eggs on objects in the water.

plate 6

banded gecko

COLEONYX VARIEGATUS

SOUTHWESTERN UNITED STATES AND NORTHERN MEXICO

The highly diversified lizards in the gecko family (Gekkonidae) are quite old on the evolutionary scale. The banded gecko is one of the more primitive family members. In the course of gecko evolution, the eyelids of most species have become transparent and immobile "contact lenses." But the banded geckos have retained the functional, opaque eyelids of their ancient relatives. The gecko tail has pre-formed breakpoints that allow it to be easily shed. A severed tail twitches wildly and helps to distract predators from the fleeing gecko. All geckos are excellent climbers, and the many different types of toe pads they have developed are a primary means of distinguishing the 90 gecko genera.

plate 7

jackson's chameleon

CHAMAELEO JACKSONI

KENYA AND TANZANIA

Although a native to the cool highlands of east Africa, a population of Jackson's chameleons has also been introduced to Hawaii. The predominately green coloration of the Jackson's chameleon allows it to blend into its native forest habitat. Three conspicuous horns on its head lend the male Jackson's chameleon the appearance of a miniature (12–14 inches) triceratops dinosaur. Chameleons are highly territorial and males use their spikes to fight off rivals. Females have only one center horn and it is much shorter than that of the male. Only the suggestion of small horns is present above the females' eyes. Jackson's is one of the few ovoviviparous chameleon species, meaning that the eggs develop in the female's body and are extruded just immediately before hatching.

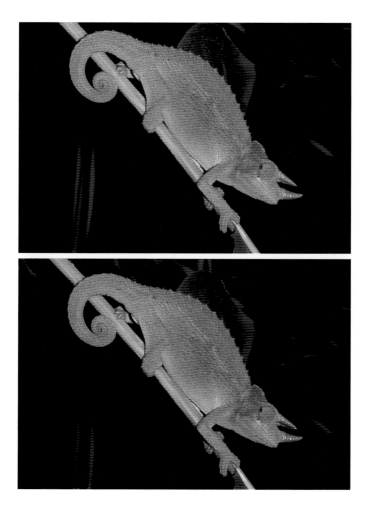

plate 8

new mexico milk snake

LAMPROPELTIS TRIANGULUM CELAENOPS

SOUTHWESTERN UNITED STATES

In this photo, a New Mexico milk snake emerges from its egg after breaking the outer shell with its egg tooth. The clear fluid is from the amnion sack, which cushions the embryo from shock. Most reptiles produce eggs that are basically closed systems. The shell is semipermeable, allowing gases and some water to pass through. Inside, a number of fluid-filled sacs perform special functions. The yolk sac provides nutrients, while other membranes allow oxygen exchange, waste storage, and cushioning. This is one of approximately 25 subspecies of *Lampropeltis triangulum*. The common name milk snake originated with one species, the eastern milk snake, which frequently visits barns in search of rodents. People mistakenly believed that these snakes entered the barns to drink cows' milk. The clear fluid is from the amnion sack, which cushions the embryo from shock. Most reptiles produce eggs that are basically closed systems. The outer layer is a leathery and somewhat pliable shell of calcareous material.

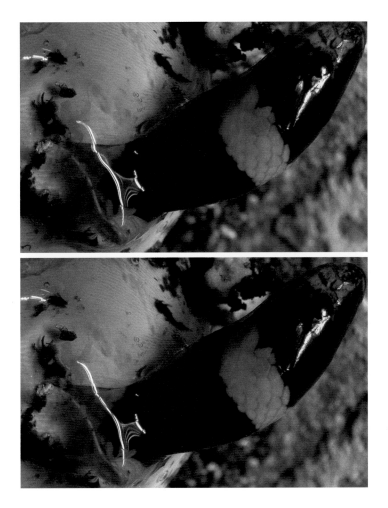

plate 9

chaco horned frog

CERATOPHRYS CRANWELLI OR ORNATA

SOUTHEASTERN SOUTH AMERICA

This odd-looking creature inspires many names, but South Americans simply refer to it as *escuerzo*, "the toad." When the short rainy season stops in the dry pampas regions of Argentina, Uruguay, and Brazil, the horned frog burrows into the ground. There it excretes a cocoonlike parchment which holds precious moisture and allows it to survive the dry season. With the return of the rains, a voracious *escuerzo* emerges to spawn and eat. Possessing a massive mouth roughly one-half the length of its enormous body, this giant frog can eat most anything. Reportedly, *escuerzo* even lures other frogs into its mouth by wiggling its toes atop its head to simulate an insect.

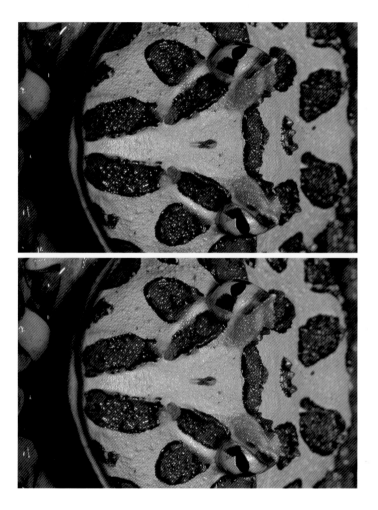

plate 10

giant leaf-tailed gecko

UROPLATUS FIMBRIATUS

MADAGASCAR

The giant leaf-tailed gecko is one of approximately 100 described species of geckos in the family Gekkonidae. Its long, strongly clawed toes are well adapted to a life in the trees. Normally, these lizards lie camouflaged on the trunk or limb of a tree, heads pointed down, defending their territory or waiting for unwary prey. They are nocturnally active, and hunt mainly for insects. The tail is not prehensile, but probably aids in balance and may store energy reserves. If it is lost, the tail regenerates, but is then plainly marked and lacks the lacy appearance of the original. The male leaf-tailed geckos are territorially aggressive towards each other, while males and females coexist peacefully.

plate 11

giant leaf-tailed gecko (close-up)

UROPLATUS FIMBRIATUS

MADAGASCAR

Most geckos lack movable eyelids, which long ago evolved into a transparent lens over the eye. Since the gecko cannot clean its eyes by blinking, it uses its tongue to do the job. The gecko relies heavily on its excellent eyesight to detect and capture fast moving insect prey. Gecko vision is adapted for motion; creatures that do not move are unlikely to be noticed and eaten. One reason for the phenomenal success of geckos is their highly specialized adaptation to nighttime activity, when insect prey is plentiful and competition is scarce.

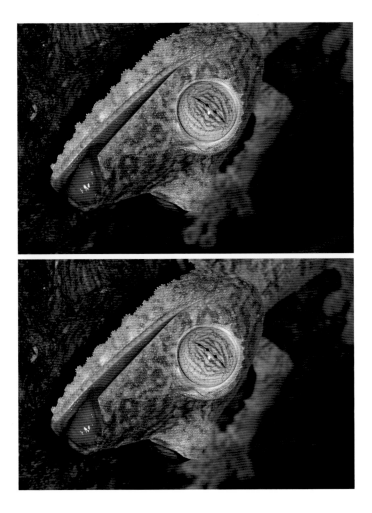

plate 12

sharp-nosed frog

RHACOPHORUS ACUTIROSTRIS

MOUNT KINABALU, BORNEO

This spectacular specimen, photographed beneath the humid jungle canopy at the 6,000 foot elevation of Mount Kinabalu, is a member of the family of brilliantly colored frogs, *Rhacophoridae*. The toes and bony heads of these *Rhacophorus* frogs are very similar to those of treefrogs (Hylidae), but skeletal differences place them in separate families. The fully webbed toes and fingers of some species of *Rhacophorus* allow them to glide up to 50 feet between trees. Most species have vertical eye slits, but in the sharp-nosed frog, they are horizontal. The 754-square kilometer Kinabalu Park is a safe haven for many animal species threatened by widespread disruption of natural habitats in the Malaysian state of Sabah.

plate 13

boa constrictor

BOA CONSTRICTOR SSP.

CENTRAL AND SOUTH AMERICA

The size, pattern, and coloring of boa constrictors varies dramatically. This species may grow to 14 feet long and weigh over 100 pounds, but the small Crawlkey boa reaches only two feet. In this photograph, the boa demonstrates how it climbs trees. In some specimens, particularly those from humid forest environments, the tail may be brightly colored. This condition has led to the common designation "red-tailed boa," but the term does not indicate a distinct species. Each snake has its own personality and some tend to bite more than others. Generally speaking, however, extending one's hand toward the head is more likely to provoke a strike. When handling a boa, the snake should be picked up in the middle with the free hand extended for the animal to use as support.

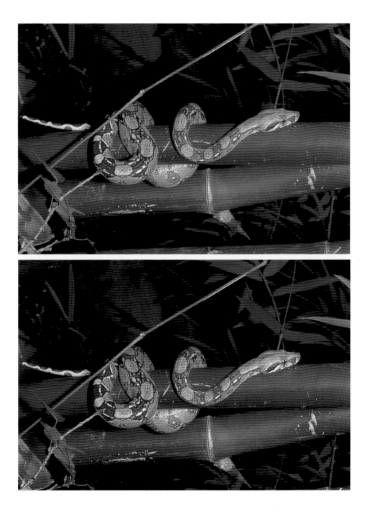

plate 14

chinese leopard gecko

GONIUROSAURUS SP.

CHINA

The highly diverse family Gekkonidae, with over 900 species and 90 genera, occupies all of the world's continents except Antarctica. One of the factors in their success is the gecko's highly specialized adaptation to nighttime activity, when insect prey is plentiful and competition is scarce. A second factor is great climbing ability. Each genera has its own specialized toe pads. Geckos in the genus *Goniurosaurus* have long, strongly clawed toes. Most geckos are insect eaters (insectivores), but larger specimens will also eat small mammals, birds, and other reptiles.

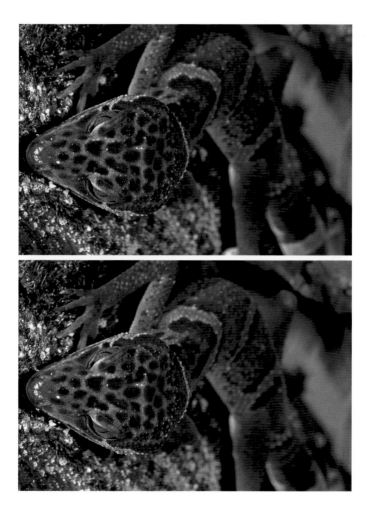

plate 15

red-eyed treefrog

AGALYCHNIS CALLIDRYAS

COSTA RICA

The scientific name of this striking rain forest jewel is derived from the Greek words for "beautiful tree nymph." An arboreal species, it lives in the forest canopy. During the evenings of the breeding season, red-eyed treefrogs descend to the pools of water on the forest floor to breed. Females carry males on their backs to suitable egg-laying sites on leaves above the pools. When the eggs hatch, the larvae drop into the water. The body of the red-eyed treefrog is slender and its fingers and toes end in disk-shaped adhesive pads that aid in tree climbing. The frog's eyes are oriented forward for binocular stereo vision. The vertical pupils are atypical for treefrogs, indicating a nocturnal lifestyle.

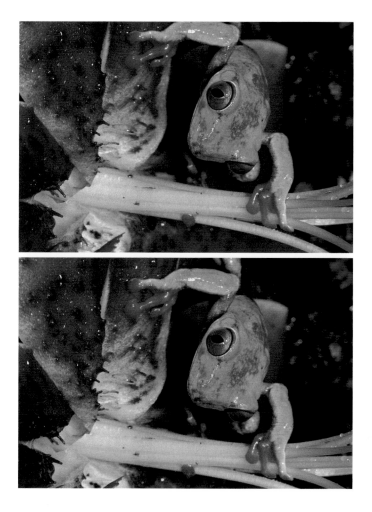

plate 16

plumed basilisk

BASILISCUS PLUMIFRONS

CENTRAL AMERICA

The large (up to two feet long) green and brown lizards in the genus *Basiliscus* occupy a relatively small range from Ecuador north to Mexico. Basilisks are arboreal reptiles and often perch on jungle branches overhanging rivers. Completely at home in the water, they can swim, dive, and hide beneath the surface. When threatened or chasing prey, the basilisk may run on its two hind legs (bipedally) at high speed. If it runs into water, a fringe on the scales of the toes is pushed up, increasing surface area and allowing the basilisk to run on water. This amazing feat has earned basilisks the nickname "Jesus lizard."

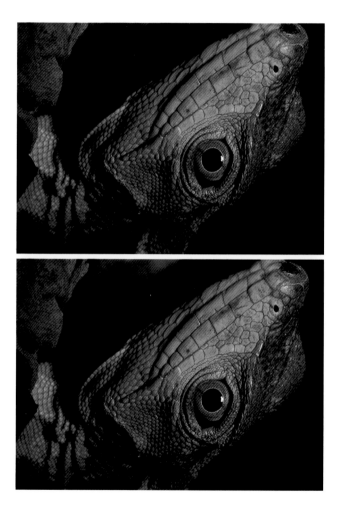

plate 17

prairie king snake

LAMPROPELTIS CALLIGASTER CALLIGASTER

CENTRAL UNITED STATES

This prairie king snake (an albino specimen) is in the process of consuming a very young mouse. As do all constrictors, this snake first tightens the coils of its body around the prey, causing death by suffocation or heart stoppage. Unable to tear its meal apart, the snake must swallow it whole, and this is most easily done head first. Snakes' jaws are hinged on special bones to open very wide, allowing them to consume objects much bigger than their own heads. The food is held in place with forward-curved teeth and pulled in by moving first one jaw and then the other forward. Because they can swallow such large prey, snakes need not eat often and many are able to survive in places such as deserts where food may be scarce.

plate 18

panther chameleon

CHAMAELEO PARDALIS

NORTHERN AND EASTERN MADAGASCAR

The ferocious behavior of this gaudy Madagascan chameleon has earned it the name "panther." This specimen is displaying an aggressive defense posture. Faced with a rival in his territory, the male panther inflates his body and turns his swollen flank towards the intruder. His normal green shade flushes a vivid red warning coloration. If this exhibition is not sufficient to drive off the encroacher, the males expose gaping mouths to each other and ultimately engage in battle. No mere skirmishes, these encounters often result in fatal wounds. A plethora of superstitions help protect Madagascar's chameleons. Touching them is considered dreadful and killing one is an ill-omen. Thus, in a culture where almost anything living is eaten, these reptiles are a dietary taboo.

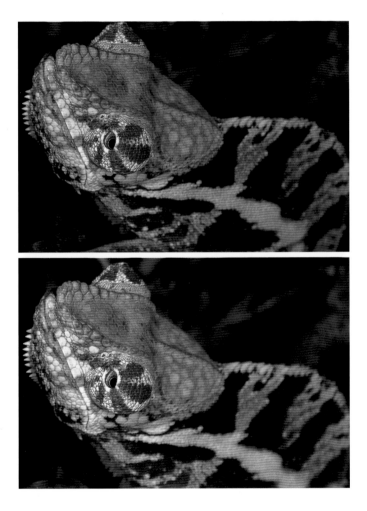

plate 19

matamata turtle

CHELUS FIMBRIATUS

NORTHERN SOUTH AMERICA

A resident of shallow pools or slow streams in the rain forests of the Amazon and Orinoco River basins, the matamata turtle lies camouflaged beneath the surface of the water. There it waits motionlessly on the bottom for unsuspecting fish to swim within the range of its wide mouth. The shell of this turtle resembles a piece of tree bark while its head and neck mimic a fallen leaf. Flaps of loose skin add to the illusion that the turtle is simply submerged forest debris. The matamata occasionally breathes by inconspicuously poking its tubelike snout out of the water.

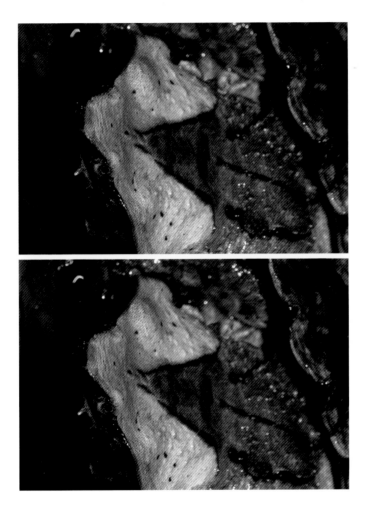

plate 20

rubber boa

CHARINA BOTTAE

WESTERN UNITED STATES

The rubber boas exhibit uniform coloration and a "rubbery" appearance that accounts for their common name. The head is short and broad with large scales on the top—an anatomical design that helps the snake to burrow. It searches underground for the small mammals and lizards that form its main diet. Like all boas, the rubber boa suffocates its prey within constricting coils. Aided by a prehensile tail, the rubber boa also climbs shrubs and trees where it may prey on small birds. A docile disposition and a moderately long captive lifespan (in excess of eleven years) make the rubber boa a popular snake for the home terrarium.

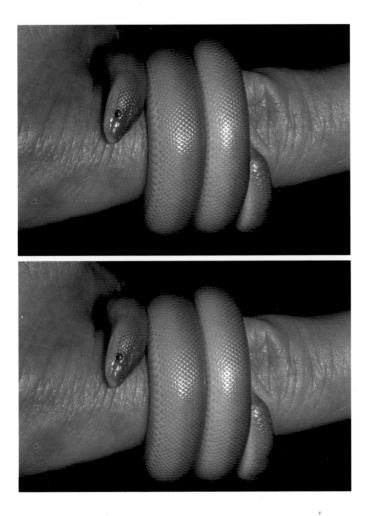

plate 21

poison-dart frog

DENDROBATES FANTASTICUS

PERU

Females of this rain forest species lay eggs in the leaf litter of the forest floor. When they hatch, the mother sits among them and a tadpole wiggles onto her back. The female then climbs into the forest canopy in search of rain water that collects inside certain plants, such as the bromeliad in this photograph. Here the tadpoles are left to develop. In most species, care of the tadpoles is left to the male, but in some species the mother returns to nourish her young with unfertilized eggs. The parents' journey far above the forest floor is difficult. Unlike treefrogs, most poison-dart frogs lack toe pads effective for climbing.

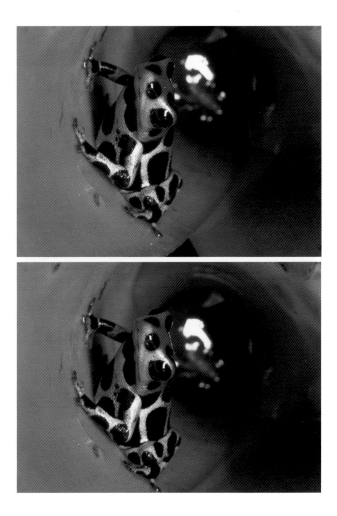

plate 22

tokay gecko

GEKKO GECKO

This large gecko is common in tropical Asia, where it frequently lives in homes, hiding in the roof by day. The tokay is welcome in the house because it voraciously consumes not only insects, but also small rodents, lizards, and snakes. As a group, geckos are the only lizards that make meaningful use of their voices, and *Gekko gecko* males are amongst the most highly vocal of all. When night falls, they can be heard chirping loudly or barking at perceived intruders. The common name "tokay" derives from the sound of one of these calls. The specimen in this photograph is displaying the next step in its progression of defensive mechanisms, the threat of a bite from its large, toothy mouth. Tokays are also quite colorful—typically bluish with orange-spot patterning.

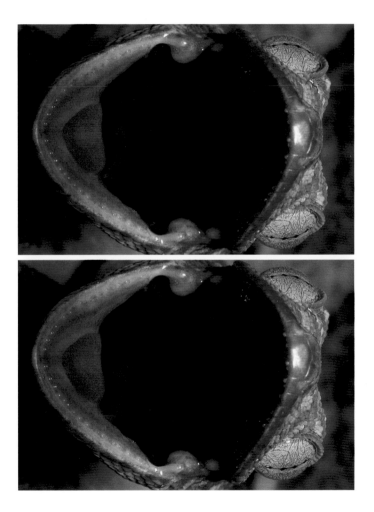

plate 23

helmeted iguana

CORYTOPHANES PERCARINATUS

MEXICO AND CENTRAL AMERICA

The lizards in the genus *Corytophanes* are close relatives of the basilisks, also in the Iguanidae family. One major difference between these lizards is that the basilisks lay eggs, while helmeted iguanas bear live young. These well-camouflaged animals are denizens of tropical rain forests from Central America to the Yucatan Peninsula. They are arboreal and feed on arthropods. Because the helmeted iguanas are active during the day, as are all Iguanids, they employ stealth and inconspicuous color patterning in order to avoid detection by prey and predators alike. The large helmet, or casque, is thought to lend this 10-inch lizard a more imposing appearance and deter attack by aggressors.

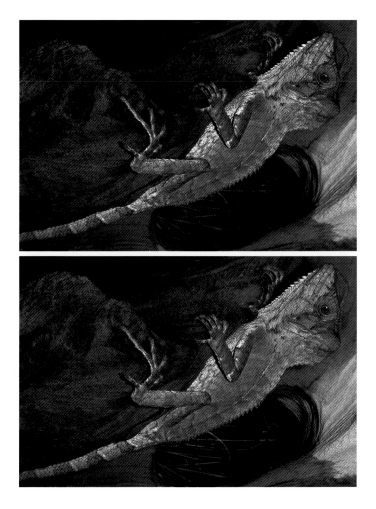

plate 24

malaysian leaf frog

MEGOPHRYS MONTANA

SOUTHEAST ASIA

The bizarre-looking Malaysian leaf frog displays excellent camouflage and is nearly invisible among the leaves on the forest floor. The frog's common name results from its leaflike appearance when seen from above. Counter-shaded color patterning disrupts its outline and unusual pointy skin flaps over the eyes further mask its presence. The Malaysian leaf frog's catlike vertical pupils indicate that it is a nocturnal creature. Although referred to as the "Malaysian" leaf frog, this four-inch species can also be found in Thailand, Sumatra, Java, and Borneo.

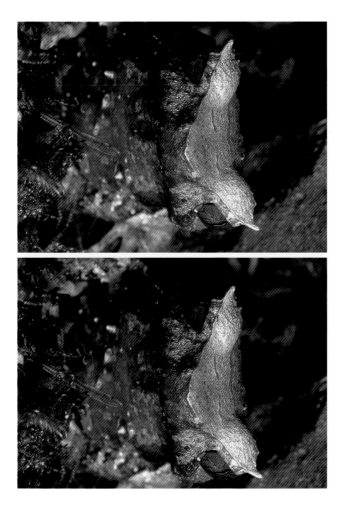

plate 25

spotted salamander

AMBYSTOMA MACULATUM

EASTERN UNITED STATES

The warmer temperatures and rains of spring signal normally shy spotted salamanders to migrate to breeding ponds, which they often share with the marbled salamander. Eggs that survive acid rain and the lethal mold Saprolegnia hatch into larva after one to two months. Over two to four months they loose their gills and metamorphose into two- to three-inch land dwellers. Leaving the ponds, the spotted salamanders seek refuge under logs, rocks, and in caves until the breeding season returns. The rarely seen adult salamanders can grow to nine inches long and live for 20 years.

plate 26

veiled chameleon (juvenile)

CHAMAELEO CALYPTRATUS

YEMEN AND SOUTHWESTERN SAUDI ARABIA

Like most chameleons from hot climates, veiled chameleons are born from eggs laid in the ground. Although chameleon embryos take quite a while to develop, the young hatchlings grow fast, with many species reaching sexual maturity in less than a year. Young chameleons immediately set out to hunt the insects which comprise their diet, and this roaming activity helps to distribute their population. The juvenile chameleons exhibit most of the behaviors of adults, but their coloration is more subdued. Compare this specimen with the mature male pictured in plate 27.

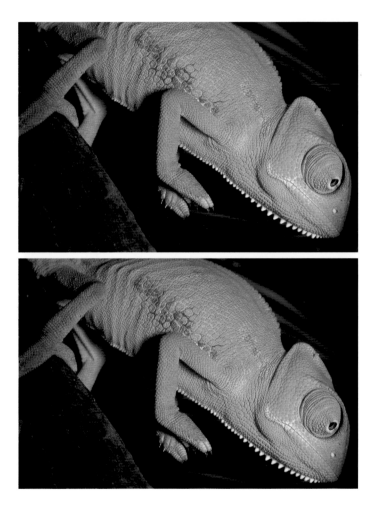

plate 27

veiled chameleon (adult)

CHAMAELEO CALYPTRATUS

YEMEN AND SOUTHWESTERN SAUDI ARABIA

The male of this large chameleon species can grow to almost two feet in length. Its brilliant coloration contrasts sharply with the veiled chameleon's drab natural habitat in the rocky steppes of Yemen and southwestern Saudi Arabia. The protrusion of the male's head, referred to as a casque, is believed to direct water condensation to the mouth, a critical adaptation to the parched Middle Eastern landscape. The imposing casque is also designed to warn off other males. Of course, the feature for which chameleons are most widely known is their remarkable ability to change color. Males are solitary and jealously guard their territory with aggressive posturing and color displays. If the intruder does not retreat, the defender will charge.

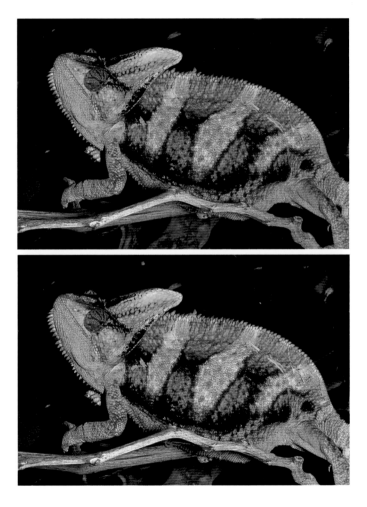

plate 28

california coastal mountain king snake

LAMPROPELTIS ZONATA MULTIFASCIATA

SANTA LUCIA MOUNTAINS, CALIFORNIA

The name of the genus *Lampropeltis* means "bright skin," a feature that helps to make mountain king snakes popular with snake enthusiasts. The three-band color pattern of these snakes strongly resembles that of poisonous coral snakes, but scientists are divided on the question of whether this similarity represents deliberate mimicry designed to trick predators into thinking that they are poisonous. Much of the evidence can be argued either way and the outcome of this debate remains uncertain. Like the milk snakes, the appearance of king snakes varies tremendously from region to region. This specimen from the Santa Lucia Mountains of Central California (the likeness of which reportedly has never previously been published) has a different appearance from the same subspecies found in the nearby Santa Cruz Mountains or the Santa Ynez Mountains.

plate 29

gecko

RHACODACTYLUS CILIATUS

NEW CALEDONIA

Most geckos are nocturnal and carnivorous insect eaters. This large Pacific island species from New Caledonia (common name unknown) may also feed on small lizards, birds, and rodents. Stealthy hunters, they approach catlike and pounce upon their prey. The victim is seized in the mouth and violently shaken or smashed into a stupor before being swallowed. The skin of the gecko is surprisingly soft to the touch. Although it is composed of scales, a feature that distinguishes reptiles from all other animals, the gecko's scales do not overlap like those of other lizards and snakes. The scales butt right up against each other and offer little resistance to the touch. This unique skin covering also lends many geckos their remarkable ability to vary their shade—usually lighter by day and darker by night.

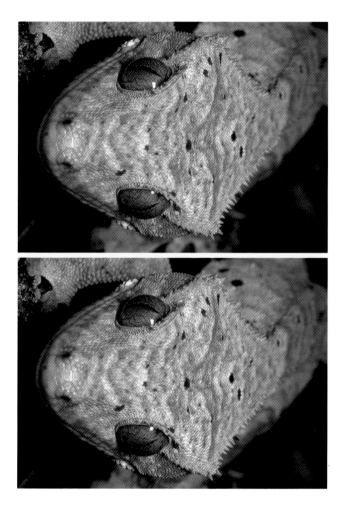

plate 30

green treefrog

HYLA CINEREA

CENTRAL AND EASTERN UNITED STATES

The acrobatic antics of treefrogs have caused them to be crowned the clowns of the amphibian world. Whether flying through the air, hanging by a toe from a slender reed or sticking upside down beneath a leaf, their movements are always comical. The gravity-defying feats of treefrogs are assisted by disklike toes and fingers visible in this photograph. These expanded pads have tremendous suction power and can cling to nearly any surface. The success of this adaptation is attested to by the existence of roughly 500 treefrog species distributed throughout the world. These prolific frogs have managed to survive and flourish in environments all the way from sea level to 15,000 feet on some of the world's highest mountains.

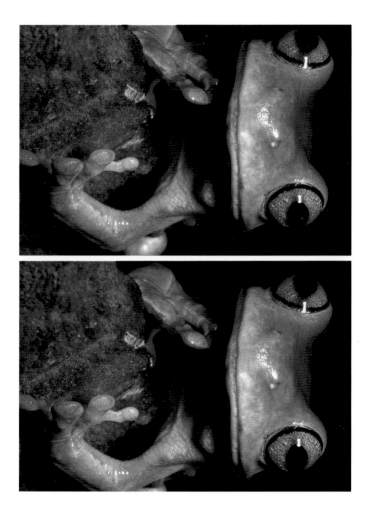

plate 31

african stumptail chameleon

RAMPHOLEON BREVICAUDATUS

TANZANIA

This miniature chameleon, about two inches long, is a fully grown adult. Residents of coastal forest areas, the tiny chameleons in this genus are distinguished from their dwarf chameleon relatives in the genus *Chamaeleo* by a shorter tail which is not prehensile. Although the African stumptail chameleons may curl their tails, they are generally not used for support, and these diminutive lizards are not strong climbers. Their tiny insectlike legs are better suited to life on or near the ground. Most species of African stumptail chameleon are dusky brown with little ability to change color. They may sit motionlessly on the forest floor for hours, indistinguishable from the leaves and rotting logs.

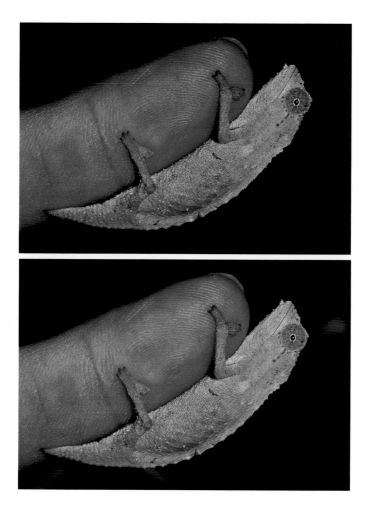

plate 32

clown treefrog

HYLA LEUCOPHYLLATA

AMAZON BASIN AND GUIANAS

This colorful treefrog occupies marshes and wetlands bordering rain forests in tropical South America. In addition to a gaudy color pattern reminiscent of a circus clown, this frog reportedly has an unusual herbal odor, although my nose was insensitive to it. Most of the world's treefrogs are placed in the genus *Hyla*. One, however, the crowned treefrog, is in the genus *Anotheca*. The clown treefrog eats insects captured with a well-aimed forward flick of its tongue. As in most frogs, the tongue is attached at the front of the mouth and free at the back, allowing it to be flung forward for some distance.

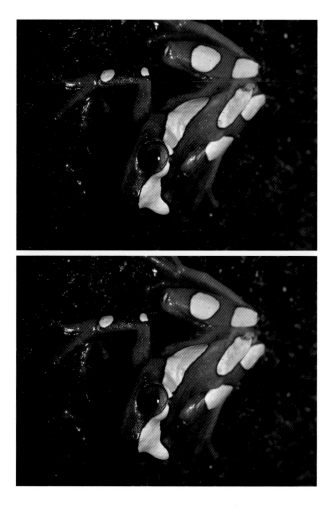

plate 33

common collared lizard

CROTAPHYTUS COLLARIS

SOUTHWESTERN UNITED STATES

This lizard gets its common name from the pair of black markings that circle the back of its neck. Males are larger (up to five inches) and more colorful than their female counterparts. Morning finds the collared lizards emerging to bask on desert rocks. With great agility and excellent eyesight, these lizards are known to seize flying insects out of the air. Like the basilisks, collared lizards can also run at high speed on their two rear legs. Males are highly territorial and aggressively defend their domain against other males. The defender arches his back and compresses his sides in a fierce push-up posture. If this display is not enough, he will chase off any intruder.

plate 34

ball python

PYTHON REGIUS

WESTERN AND CENTRAL AFRICA

This is a typical posture for the small (about three feet long) and reclusive ball python, with its head held over its coils. The pits visible below the mouth are temperature-sensitive organs that help this nocturnal snake on its nighttime hunt for rodent prey. All pythons are egg layers (oviparous) and are found mostly in the Old World. Female pythons positively dote on their developing eggs, caring for them until they are ready to hatch. The mother snake coils around the eggs and incubates them in a burrow or nest that she creates. If the temperature drops too low, she will shiver to generate a stable heat. The female will only leave her brood to drink water or bask her cold-blooded body in the sun. She will not eat while brooding and may lose up to one-half her body weight.

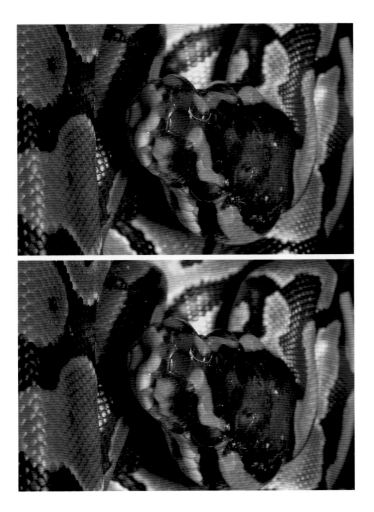

plate 35

giant day gecko

PHELSUMA MADAGASCARIENSIS GRANDIS

MADAGASCAR

Geckos in the genus *Phelsuma* of the Madagascar region are distinguished from most other species by their daytime (diurnal) activity and vivid green coloration. Green skin probably helps the giant day gecko to blend into its leafy natural habitat and lessens detection by predators during the day. If the lizard is caught, its beaded skin tears easily and helps the lizard to escape. Day geckos are extremely agile and excellent jumpers. They have also developed a specialized flight mechanism. When faced with a predatory threat such as an approaching raptor, the lizard may release from its perch in the trees and fall into the foliage below. Using its tail for balance, the gecko always manages to land catlike on its feet. At least two dozen species of day gecko are identified on Madagascar alone. This species has an especially loud froglike voice, and is commonly found on coconut palms.

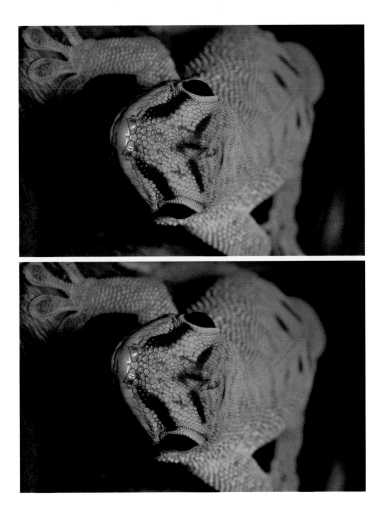

plate 36

panther chameleon (feeding)

CHAMAELEO PARDALIS

NOSSI BÉ MADAGASCAR

This panther chameleon from Nossi Bé, an island off the north coast of Madagascar, demonstrates the extraordinary chameleon tongue in action. First the reptile's two eyes are swiveled forward to locate the prey stereoscopically and to aim the head. Next, the unique musculature of the tongue flashes forward—up to an amazing body length and a half in as little as 1/100th of a second. Nine times out of ten the sticky tongue tip hits the insect, gripping it tightly in an abrasive sheath. When contact is made, tendons arrest the tongue's forward motion and a set of accordionlike retractor muscles draw it back into a resting place in the throat. As soon as the tongue is pulled in, the chameleon mechanically begins to chew, even if it has missed the target prey.

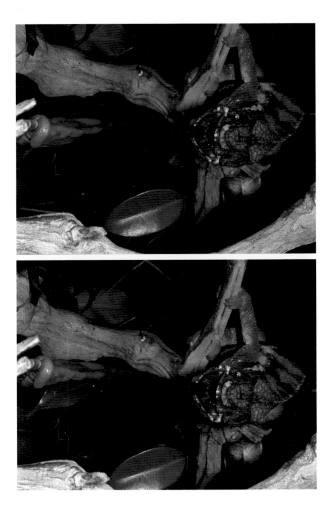

plate 37

pacific treefrog

HYLA REGILLA

WESTERN UNITED STATES INTO BRITISH COLUMBIA

The loud, droning chorus of this little frog is so commonly recognized that Hollywood filmmakers often incorporate it into soundtracks in order to evoke the effect of an outdoor evening. Not actually a tree climber, the Pacific treefrog is found on the ground and in shrubs wherever the ground is wet, from sea level to 10,000 feet in elevation. *Regilla* is the chameleon of frogs, capable of quick and dramatic color changes, from a monotone dark brown to bright green and bronze with a complicated array of markings.

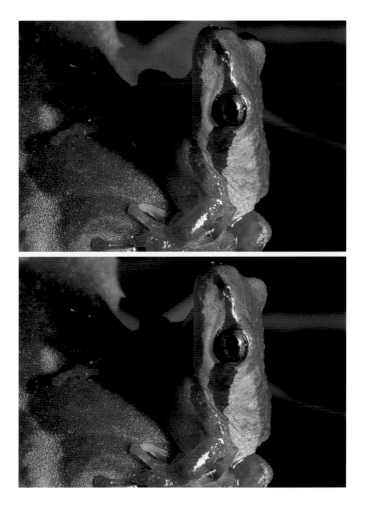

plate 38

leopard gecko

EUBLEPHARIS MACULARIUS

SOUTHWEST ASIA

The delicate appearance of these gentle lizards belies their harsh native environments. From the dry desert mountains of Afghanistan and Pakistan to East India, they have been found at nearly 7,000 feet in elevation. Both sexes have thick tails (probably to store fat and other nutrients), but the tail of the male is more bulbous. It breaks off easily and, as in other lizards, regrows in a different shape and color. The adult males are highly territorial and skirmishes are common, especially during the seven- to eight-month breeding season. These long-lived lizards have been kept in captivity for up to 22 years. Females may produce several clutches of two eggs each, which hatch in roughly 55 days. The temperatures to which the eggs are subjected, not genetics, determine the sex of the gecko hatchling.

plate 39

nile monitor

VARANUS NILOTICUS SSP.

AFRICA

The largest of the African monitors, this species grows to six feet in length. Monitor lizards are confined to the Old World (Australia, Asia, and Africa). All monitors are egg layers and active during the day (diurnal). The Nile monitor favors moist environments and females often lay eggs in nests excavated in termite mounds with their powerful reptilian claws. The adult monitors do not guard the eggs, but may return to excavate the eggs from the mound after they are hatched.

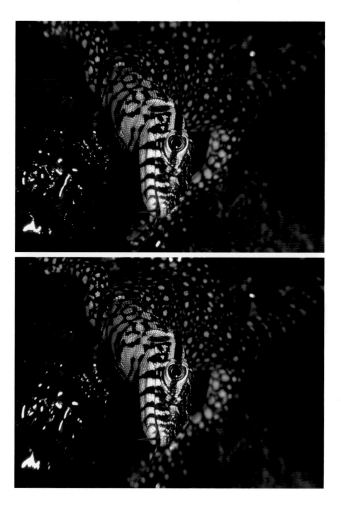

plate 40

gray treefrog tadpole

HYLA CHRYSOSCELIS OR VERSICOLOR

CENTRAL AND EASTERN UNITED STATES

This specimen is one of two possible species of gray treefrog which cannot be distinguished except in the laboratory. The oval-shaped bodies of the frog larvae are commonly referred to as tadpoles, a term that originally meant "toadhead." Most are plant eating (herbivorous), but some eat other animals (carnivorous). The period of tadpole metamorphosis into a frog varies from days to months, and in the case of the American bullfrog, may take one or two years. Gray treefrog tadpoles emerge from the water a bright shade of emerald green, which may help to camouflage them in algae-filled ponds. Adults sport warty skin that rapidly changes from brown to greenish gray. These color shifts may be induced by changes in both light and temperature.

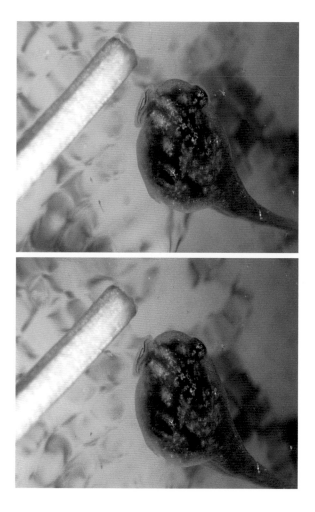

plate 41

hawksbill sea turtle

ERETMOCHELYS IMBRICATA

ALL TROPICAL SEAS

Although theoretically found in all tropical seas, exploitation of the hawksbill turtle has led to its disappearance in numerous locations. This specimen was photographed off the shore of Sipadan Island, Borneo. Around the world, the hawksbill turtle is known as the "tortoiseshell turtle" for its beautiful carapace, highly prized in the manufacture of combs, brushes, etc. This dubious honor has put extreme harvesting pressure on the hawksbill for centuries. They are also threatened by loss of nesting habitat and hunting of the turtles and their eggs for human consumption, often illegally. Today, hawksbill turtle populations remain in grave jeopardy.

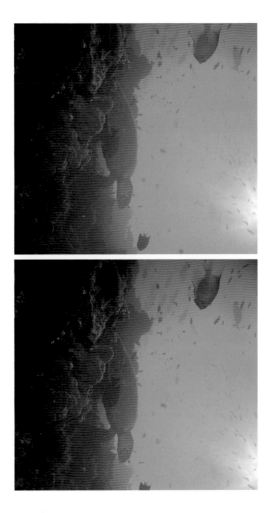

plate 42

white's treefrog

LITORIA CAERULEA

AUSTRALIA AND NEW GUINEA

Known as the green treefrog in Australia, a rotund body with rolls of skin above the ear covering (tympanum) have gained this amphibian the popular nickname "dumpy frog." Remarkably, despite its large size (nearly six inches), this treefrog is an adept climber. Large adhesive toe pads help it to seek out prey wherever it may be found. White's treefrog is exceptionally tolerant of people and frequents human habitations, where it seeks out food (insects and small rodents) and moisture. Scientists at the University of Adelaide have reported that compounds in the frog's skin can lower human blood pressure and attack cold sore viruses and staph bacteria.

plate 43

albino corn snake

ELAPHE GUTTATA SSP.

CENTRAL AND EASTERN UNITED STATES

This constrictor preys heavily on rats, mice, birds, and bats. American farmers especially appreciate its role in controlling rodent populations. Some say that the common name "corn snake" stems from the snake's habit of entering corn cribs in search of rodents. Others believe the name was gained from the similarity of the belly markings to the checked pattern on Indian corn kernels. Whatever the origins of its name, however, the corn snake is undisputedly one of the most beautiful snakes in the United States. This specimen is a captive-bred albino.

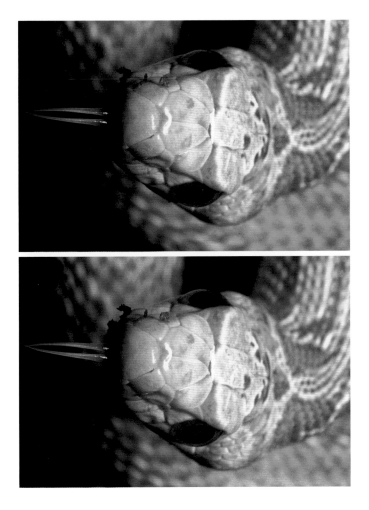

plate 44

orange and black poison-dart frog

DENDROBATES LEUCOMELAS

VENEZUELA

This species of Dendrobatid frog is considered to be one of approximately 55 toxic species of poison-dart frogs. Vibrant colors probably display a warning to potential predators that the frog may be poisonous. The toxicity of wild poison-dart frogs gradually diminishes in captivity. Froglets born of captive parents are completely nonpoisonous. The loss of toxic secretions may be due to a change in diet. If so, this suggests that the alkaloid poisons secreted by these frogs may possibly come from wild insects that are absent from the diets of captive specimens.

glossary

An **alkaloid** is an organic substance that is generally poisonous, but in some circumstances may have medicinal effects.

Amphibians are cold-blooded, smooth-skinned vertebrates in the class Amphibia. They typically hatch as aquatic larvae, breathing by means of gills, then metamorphose into adults that breathe air with lungs.

Arboreal animals live primarily in trees.

An **arthropod** is any member of the phylum arthropoda that includes insects, crustaceans, and arachnids.

Camouflage is a means of concealment by which an animal matches the appearance of its natural surroundings.

A **carapace** is a hard, bony, protective outer covering.

Carnivorous animals are flesh eaters and often predators.

A **casque** is a helmetlike structure or armor covering the head.

Class is a category used to classify animals. Order, family, genus, and species are other categories of biological classification ranking below class.

Clutch refers to a number of eggs produced or incubated all at one time.

Desert regions inhabited by reptiles and amphibians are typically dry and sandy, and are marked by relatively extreme temperature changes, supporting little vegetation and a limited, specially adapted animal population.

An **embryo** is an organism in the early stages of its development, before it has reached a distinctly recognizable form.

Genus is a category of biological classification, ranking below the family and above the species.

A **hatchling** is a newborn animal that has just emerged from its egg.

Herpetology is the zoological study of reptiles and amphibians.

Incubation is a means of warming eggs by bodily heat to bring about development of embryos.

Larva is the earliest, newly hatched stage of an animal or insect that undergoes metamorphosis, noticeably different in form from its adult stage.

Mimicry is the resemblance through natural selection of one organism to another, or to a natural object, as an aid in concealment.

Montane plants and animals grow in and inhabit mountainous regions.

A **morph** refers to a specific variation of form, shape, or color of an animal.

Nocturnal animals are active mostly at night.

An **opaque** covering does not allow light to pass through it.

Opposable digits, such as thumbs, face opposite other fingers or toes and are useful for grasping and holding objects.

Order is a category for the classification of living things, below the class and above the family.

A **parasite** is a living thing that feeds off another organism while living on or inside it, often harming the host animal in the process.

A **predator** is an animal that captures and eats other animals; this behavior is described as predation.

Prehensile means adapted for holding or seizing by wrapping around an object.

A **reptile** is a cold-blooded, usually egg-laying vertebrate of the class Reptilia, having an outer covering of scales or horny plates and breathing with lungs.

To **secrete** is to produce a substance from bodily fluids.

A **species** is a group of plants or animals that breed with one another and share physical characteristics.

A **tadpole** is the aquatic larval stage of a frog or toad, with a tail and external gills that disappear as its limbs develop and it reaches its adult stage.

A **terrarium** is a closed container or enclosure used for growing small plants or keeping small animals such as turtles, lizards, snakes, or frogs.

A **toxin** is a poisonous substance.

Tropical regions, located just above and just below the Earth's equator, have higher average temperatures and less seasonal temperature change than other areas, making for a relatively consistent hot and humid climate.

A **vertebrate** is an animal that has a backbone or spinal column.

index

about the author

MARK BLUM has been photographing the natural world in 3-D for three decades, both as a stock photographer and on assignment. He has designed much of his own equipment to meet the special challenges of stereoscopic wildlife photography. This volume is Mark's fifth 3-D book, including *Beneath the Sea in 3-D* and *Bugs in 3-D* for Chronicle Books. His stereophotography has also been published in magazines, on CD-ROM, and on ViewMaster® reels under a Discovery Channel® license. In commemoration of the Year of the Ocean, Mark's underwater 3-D images were projected onto a specially installed 41-foot screen for thousands of viewers attending the Expo '98 World Fair in Lisbon, Portugal. Mark makes his home on the Monterey Bay in California. (Email: markb@redshift.com; Web site: www.redshift.com/~markb)